Midbrain and The Beast

A Family Guide and Client Workbook

By: Dallas W. Bennett

Over the past twenty years while working as a substance abuse counselor and helping people who struggle with drug and alcohol addiction, [some making it and some not] I've learned a few things about what works and what doesn't. During the last few years I've been focusing most of my efforts toward something I feel is very important to long term success. And the success I'm referring to means a lot more than just sobriety.

Anyone can quit drinking and drugging. A ten year old child can tell you how to quit drinking and drugging. Quitting is the easy part. Staying clean and sober; that's the difficult part. The biggest challenge for most people is living life on life's terms without turning to a mood altering chemical. And how to do that is what I'm going to share with you in this book.

We'll get into the details of what separates the winners from the losers. Some people don't like when I use the word loser. However, the reality is, if you relapse you will increase your chances of losing this game called life. If you want to be successful do what successful people do, go where they go and learn what they learn. Successful people in recovery are willing to do what the unsuccessful people won't do. This separates the men from the boys [the mature women from the little girls].

As you read this small book you'll notice I like to keep things simple. I do it this way mainly so I can understand it and then explain things in a way you can understand it. Then you can gain the knowledge and apply it to your life. We've all heard that knowledge is power. Well, I've learned that applied knowledge is real power. And power means the ability to make things happen; to get something done. So, let's get started.

Chapter 1:

The Rebellious Road to Destruction

One of the main reasons you originally used drugs and alcohol is because you had a spiritual problem. In other words you were not content with how you felt about your life at that point so you decided to use an outside substance to alter your mood. Every person on the planet uses drugs and alcohol for one reason; to change their mood. You wouldn't use the substance if it didn't change your mood - make you feel better or help you not feel.

Deep down in your heart you know it's wrong to smoke crack, shoot heroin, take more pain pills than your doctor prescribed and ignore the dangerous risk of drinking and driving. So what did you do? You listen to that voice inside telling you to just do it anyway. It's called a rebellious spirit.

Some of you just wanted to get high or drunk. You ignored all common sense and parental wisdom and followed the desires of your youth and rebelled. You wanted to "do your thing" and you did it. It didn't matter who it hurt and how much shame it caused your family.

Some of you were emotionally hurt and tried to find relief in drugs and alcohol. You were probably given an opportunity to talk with someone but your pride convinced you to clam-up and not share your feelings with people that care about you. This kind of pride is a form of rebellion. It's like saying; "I don't need help. I hurt inside but leave me alone I'll be just fine. I can do this by myself."

And some of you got hurt physically and decide to use more than intended. Either way its rebellion and that's a spiritual problem. Some of you can remember your parents or grandparents telling you to stay away from those kinds of friends. You were warned at every corner in life encouraging you to say no to drugs.

A rebellious spirited person won't listen. They'll say something like, "stop telling me what to do. That's your problem; you're always trying to tell me what to do. Why don't you get off my back? I don't need your help."

When a person gives into this rebellious spirit they'll start producing certain fruit. The fruit of rebellion looks something like this: stubbornness, bull-headedness, bitterness, judgmental, faultfinding, agitation, frustration, gossip, defiance, grandiosity and ungratefulness.

If you're using drugs and alcohol and you continue in your rebellious state you'll begin to misuse drugs and alcohol. It will not take very long and you'll start walking down the road to addiction. As you move down this road you'll eventually come to the next stage called abuse.

We understand abuse as a psychological problem. When you start abusing drugs and alcohol you'll start having all kinds of psychological issues. You'll start feeling sad, depressed, angry, mad, hopeless, anxious, hateful and resentful. You'll also start lying, cheating, acting sneaky, manipulating and conning. If you keep abusing, you'll also start experiencing personal feelings of shame, guilt, self-condemnation, poor self-esteem and worthlessness.

As you continue to follow this rebellious spirit, along with your new found psychological problems, denial seems to develop a stronger root system. Most people at this point begin to spiral quickly down the road of addiction to the final stage: chemical dependency. (Addiction)

We understand chemical dependence as a biological problem. Somewhere down the road you will eventually cross this invisible line called addiction. It's a little different for everyone because of our individual chemical makeup. Some people take longer to damage their brain and other people screw it up quickly. When you abuse that area of your brain for long periods of time with outside substances it can cause lifelong medical problems to an organ in your body: Your Brain.

When you cross the line of addiction it is no longer just a spiritual or psychological problem. It's now also biological. At this point you will demonstrate animalistic and survival behaviors; mainly because the midbrain (beast brain) is in control. The symptoms may look like; uncontrollable physical cravings, suicidal thoughts, extreme risky behaviors, abandon family, will not eat, and ignore morals and values. You will disregard your inner core belief system to answer the internal beasts call for more drugs or alcohol based on the depletion of natural chemicals caused by substance use/abuse/dependence.

At this point, you've moved so far down the road of addiction it has now become what we call a bio-psycho-social-spiritual problem. You need to deal with all of them at the same time but focus on the biological part first. You have to arrest the physical craving (beast) before you can deal with the psychological issues. That means abstaining from all mood altering chemicals.

I must accept the fact I cannot drink or drug
like everyone else, make a commitment to abstinence
and move on with my life
Or
I will go back into the laboratory of life,
conduct some more drinking and drugging experiments,
cause some more pain and shame
and hopefully prove to myself
I cannot drink or drug like everyone else.

Chapter 2:

The Neurobiology of Addiction

Learning Goals:

1. To understand the biological part of addiction. This will expose your true enemy within and reduce a significant amount of shame.

2. To finally realize "why" you continue to do things that hurt yourself and your family even though you really don't want to.

3. To gain knowledge about how each different neurotransmitter chemical is effected by using and abusing drugs and alcohol.

4. To answer the question of why you couldn't say no to that invisible magnet pulling you and making you do what you promised you would never do again?

ASAM - Definition of Addiction:

(American Society of Addiction Medicine)

Addiction is a primary, chronic disease of brain reward, motivation, memory and related circuitry. Dysfunction in these circuits leads to characteristic biological, psychological, social and spiritual manifestations. This is reflected in an individual pathologically pursuing reward and/or relief by substance use and other behaviors.

Have you ever asked yourself one or both of these two questions?

1. Why do I continue using and hurting myself and my family even though I really don't want to do it?

2. Why can't I say no to this invisible magnet pulling me and making me do things I promised I would never do again?

If you've never asked yourself one of these questions, and you keep using drugs, give it a little while and you'll eventually ask yourself one or both of these questions.

If you have asked yourself one or both of these questions, hang on and allow me to explain.

Basically, your brain is made of two parts; a top part and a bottom part. The top part of your brain is called the neocortex; the Real You. The bottom part of your brain is called the midbrain; the animalistic part of your brain. We refer to this as your Beast Brain.

Neocortex: (Real You)

The neocortex allows you to be conscious, to think rational, understand language, to control your voluntary muscles, to solve abstract problems and have consequential thinking in which to plan for your future in order to reach short and long term goals.

Your neocortex is "the real you," and you are capable of overcoming any desire, even for oxygen or food. Your voluntary muscles (hands, feet, etc.) are "supported" directly to your neocortex -- to the real you.

The real you (neocortex) originally did not want to use drugs. It had no desire to get caught up in the stressful consequences of addiction. It never did. The Real You (neocortex) wants to be a good parent and spouse, a productive member of society and live a healthy productive life with joy and peace.

Midbrain: (The Beast)

Your midbrains primary mission is to keep you alive. It's built for one reason – survival.

The midbrain is where you get the uncontrollable desire to drink water and eat food so that you can stay alive. It controls the automatic functions of your body; it keeps your heart beating, lungs breathing and eyes blinking.

Your midbrain beast is essentially helpless, unable to get what it wants, unless you give it what it thinks it needs. Drugs and alcohol warp or twist the function of the midbrain's real survival needs.

Once you start abusing drugs and alcohol it distorts the midbrain and eventually makes people feel willing do most anything to continue the use of that substance -- even if it means the loss of everything else that is important. The midbrain "Beast" is ruthless, cunning and baffling in getting what it thinks it needs to survive.

Midbrain Chemicals

(Neurotransmitters)

These chemicals are stored in a small organ located near the bottom of your midbrain. In order to keep this simple we'll call this organ a pump. It looks similar to a bulb used to clean out a baby's nose. This pump is full of different chemicals. These chemicals give you feelings.

Basically, most everything you experience in life stimulates this pump. The pump releases chemicals and gives you a feeling. The feelings are everything from A to Z; anger, happiness, sadness, pleasure, anxiety, excitement, etc....

God intended for you to experience all these emotions when he created your midbrain pump. He wanted you to have fun, be adventurous, cry, laugh, and enjoy life within the parameters of goodness and without moving into unhealthy desires. He also wanted you to feel sad and angry at times. Sadness is part of the grieving process and anger is normal emotion too. He wanted you to be a human being full of emotions.

Listed below are seven chemicals and the normal feelings they should give you. Let's now look at a these chemicals and how they were designed to work in life.

Chemical	Feelings
Dopamine	Pleasure and Reward
Serotonin	Calmness, Sleep, Sadness
Endorphin	Pain Relief
GABA	Anti-Anxiety
Epinephrine	Anger, Fear, Fight or Flight,
PIP	Caring, Love, Relationship
Acetylcholine	Perception, Movement, and Memory

Dopamine:

Dopamine is released when you catch a big fish, watch your son slide into second base, cheer for your favorite team when they score the winning point, listen to your daughter sing at a Christmas play, ride a roller coaster, eat good food, have sex and do most anything that brings you pleasure and gives you a sense of reward.

Serotonin:

Serotonin is released as you start getting sleepy. The release of this chemical is how we all go to sleep. It's also released when you have a need to calm down, relax and feel sad.

Endorphin:

Endorphins are released when you experience pain. If you hit your finger with a hammer it'll cause pain and then your midbrain releases endorphins to help reduce the pain as much as possible. Runners understand about the runners high or the second wind. The exercise is causing enough pain to release more endorphins which numbs the pain helping you run further and/or faster.

GABA:

GABA is released when you need to calm down before or after a stressful, traumatic or scary situation. This chemical prevents you from having an anxiety or panic attack.

Epinephrine:

Epinephrine is basically adrenaline. This chemical gives you the feelings of anger, fear, fight or flight. If a snake surprised you in the woods your midbrain would release this chemical and you would either run, pick up a stick and fight or become frozen with fear.

PIP:

PIP is an acronym for a chemical that gives you the feelings of caring, love and relationship. This does not necessary always mean romantic feelings toward your spouse or girlfriend. It could also mean the feelings you have for other family members, close friends and opportunities to demonstrate compassion.

Acetylcholine:

Acetylcholine is released to help you with perception, movement and memory. It gives you the correct feelings of balance and how fast or slow you may be going.

Let's now look at how drugs and alcohol can damage your midbrain pump by releasing abnormal amounts of the natural chemicals and depleting your midbrain pump.

Whenever you do something natural that stimulates your pump, it releases a chemical and gives you a feeling. After the chemical is released and you experience the feeling, your pump will quickly fill back up. It's designed to replenish itself immediately.

Whenever you put drugs and alcohol into your system your pump releases an abnormal amount of chemicals. It's like taking one step forward and two steps backward.

If you continue using drugs and alcohol your pump will eventually start depleting. It'll get lower and lower until your midbrain starts feeling like it can't function as a normal human being. Your midbrain will then attempt to drive you to do what you promised to never do again just to get that chemical feeling back to normal.

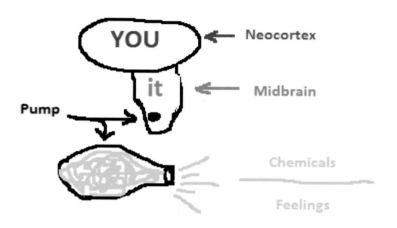

Chemicals   **(Drugs Releasing Abnormal Amounts)**

Chemicals	Drugs Releasing Abnormal Amounts
Dopamine	Cocaine, Alcohol, Meth, Nicotine, (Porn)
Serotonin	Alcohol, Benzodiazepine, Marijuana
Endorphin	Opiates, Nicotine, (Self-Mutilation)
GABA	Cocaine, Meth, Ecstasy, Benzodiazepine
Epinephrine	Meth, Cocaine, Alcohol
PIP	Cocaine, Meth, Alcohol,
Acetylcholine	Marijuana, Benzodiazepine, Alcohol

Dopamine:

Cocaine releases an unnatural amount of this chemical. The first time a person uses crack it releases the amount of dopamine as if a person had a 10 minute orgasm. It never reaches that amount again. Methamphetamine and alcohol also release too much dopamine. The initial alcohol buzz comes from dopamine. If you keep abusing drugs the pump will slowly become depleted of dopamine, tolerance will go up and the midbrain will take control of the rational top part of your brain and make you go get more drugs to try and fill that dopamine level back up to normal.

Serotonin:

Alcohol releases an unnatural amount of this chemical. As mentioned earlier the buzz comes from the dopamine. But it's followed by major amounts of serotonin. That's why you pass out; you're getting an overload of serotonin. Remember, serotonin makes you go to sleep. You're actually going into a coma, the first stages of death. If you keep abusing alcohol the pump will slowly become depleted of serotonin, tolerance will go up, depression kicks in and the midbrain will take control of the rational top part of your brain and make you go get more alcohol to try and fill that serotonin level back up to normal.

Endorphin:

Opioids releases this chemical. If you're abusing pain pills or heroin, your pump will release abnormal amounts of endorphins and start depleting the pump of this chemical. Nicotine and self-mutilation will also effect this chemical and create strong cravings and high tolerance. If you keep abusing opiates the pump will slowly become depleted of endorphins, tolerance will go up and the midbrain will take control of the rational top part of your brain and make you go get more opiates to try and fill that endorphin level back up to normal.

GABA:

Cocaine and Meth releases an unnatural amount of this chemical. Abusing benzodiazepine will also deplete the GABA. When this chemical is low you can have anxiety and panic attacks. Abusing any of these three drugs may cause a serious depletion of GABA and can lead to paranoia. When this happens you will begin to see things and hear things that are not real.

Epinephrine:

Meth, cocaine and alcohol releases an unnatural amount of this chemical. Meth will make most people wired with so much of this chemical they feel like fighting. For some people alcohol will also produce more of this chemical and cause people to fight. A lot of people have anger problems caused by abnormal amounts of epinephrine.

PIP:

Cocaine, Meth and alcohol releases too much of this chemical. When the pump gets low of PIP you'll begin to lose your ability to care for others. You can deplete this chemical so low that you will not care about anything important to you like your career, freedom, sanity, and even your own family. Your beast brain will drive you like an animal to get more drugs.

Acetylcholine:

Marijuana and alcohol release too much of this chemical. Smoking pot over time will cause you to get low of Acetylcholine. You'll start losing your memory and your motor skills will slow down. I call this the Cheech and Chong syndrome: Old pot users forget what day it is and they struggle with concentration. When this chemical is low you can't keep a job or be the parent/spouse you need to be.

One last thought about the midbrain:

You need to understand your midbrain really doesn't care about the drugs and alcohol. It wants the chemical rush from the unnatural release of neurotransmitters in your pump. And once that pump gets to a certain depletion level it (The Beast Brain) will try to make you go get what it thinks it needs to survive. The midbrain "feels" like it can't function as a normal human being. It really feels like it's going to die. That feeling is in the same area of the brain as if you went 3 days without water or 30 days without food. It's being tricked and it's trying to survive.

The good news is the midbrain pump will most often fill back up with the normal chemicals it needs to function correctly. This replenishing process takes most people 6 to 12 months. This is why it's important to have a strong aftercare plan and an understanding of the post-acute withdrawal syndrome. Your toughest battle during the first year is your midbrain (physical).

For as long as you're a human being your midbrain will always remember what it feels like to have an abundance of chemicals rushing through your body. Those strong desires from the physical (midbrain) will stick its ugly head up from time to time and tempt you with thoughts, feelings and imaginations. You must learn how to combat this midbrain desire and silence your beast.

Chapter 3:

Silence the Beast

Your Beast brain is cunning and baffling. Have you ever tried to stop using, then relapsed, later regretted it and then thought, "Why did I do that?" You fell for the sabotaging of your midbrain. It starts out as a small seemingly innocent thought, which leads to another, and then another until it snowballs into something that you find very difficult to stop or control. It can eventually drive you to act like an animal.

However, the midbrain is not really your enemy. We would all die without it. It controls the automatic functions of our body. It gives us the <u>desire or cravings</u> for food, water, and sex: The survival needs. It also keeps us breathing, our heart beating, eyes blinking and instincts working. The real you (neocortex) has no desire to use. It never did. You want to be a good parent, a productive member of society and live life with happiness joy and peace.

You can train yourself to use the RAT technique and combat the thoughts, feelings, and imaginations to use drugs. Here is the definition of your BEAST:

Any thought, feeling or imagination that causes you to think about using any mood altering chemical.

Here's the bad news: Your midbrain has been permanently reprogrammed to try and trick you into using, and will do so for the rest of your life. As long as you are a human being, and you have a brain, you will always remember what it feels like to have an abundance of chemical rushing in your midbrain and giving you that un-natural high feeling. You can be tempted at any time. Especially during the first six months to a year while your midbrain chemical pump is filling back up. Remember it takes the average person 6-12 months to balance out in their emotions.

Here's the good news: The real you (your neocortex) is in charge. You have to give permission for your midbrain to use the drugs it wants – you are in control -- not it! Even though 10 years from now your midbrain will still want to GET HIGH, its voice will get less and less enticing and persuasive as you resist it, allowing your midbrain pump to fill up as you work your recovery program.

For some people, gaining this knowledge helps with the process of letting go of guilt or shame. Now you should see that the reason you have thoughts or dreams of using is not because you aren't moral enough or religious enough or strong enough. It's because you are human. All humans have these brains. Any human being that experiences a mood altering substance to the point of reaching an unnatural high, or excessive euphoric effect, will cause a malfunction in their midbrain pump. The extreme release of the pleasure chemicals (dopamine, endorphin, etc.) will permanently alter anyone's brain. Like a 110 watt fan being plugged into 220 power outlet, it will run very fast for a short while and then break - damage has been done. Don't trust your best thinking – it's broken! Do you now see that your problem is not that you don't have enough will power, moral character, or internal strength? It's more a biological problem – and also social and psychological.

So what's the solution? Don't wait for the desire to go away - most of the time it doesn't! Take action now even though you don't feel like it. This is where self-discipline kicks in and most people don't have enough? Admit it, you don't have enough! Not on your own anyway. Most people that are successful in recovery were: (1) smart enough to realize and accept this and (2) made the choice to humble themselves in order to receive the help they need from others.

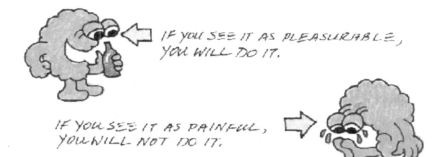

IF YOU SEE IT AS PLEASURABLE, YOU WILL DO IT.

IF YOU SEE IT AS PAINFUL, YOU WILL NOT DO IT.

Here are 5 ways to silence your beast:

I encourage you to learn the RAT relapse prevention technique. This is a skill you can use to combat the thoughts, feelings and imaginations trying to persuade you to use again.

RAT – Recognize Addictive Thinking

How do you recognize when your midbrain is trying to get you to drink or use drugs? Whenever you have any thought, feeling or imagination trying to get you to use – that's coming from your midbrain Beast. The key is recognition. Once you recognize it at this level you can easily combat it using this skill. This is not a craving skill. If you're craving it's probably too late. I'm teaching you how to catch it when it's just a thought, feeling or imagination.

Here is the definition of the BEAST once again: Any *thought*, *feeling* or *imagination* that causes you to think about using any mood altering chemical.

Five techniques to silence the BEAST:

1- Prayer
2- Call Someone
3- Play the movie to the end
4- Count backwards from 100
5- Exercise

I want to encourage you to memorize each of these 5 techniques. Allow me to explain each technique and how it can help you silence your midbrain beast.

1- **Prayer:** Some people won't pray because they think they don't know how to pray. Prayer basically means to communicate one to another. You can say the serenity prayer or just talk with God or your higher power. The science community has proven that prayer is good for us and makes us feel better. Just talk with God and tell him how you feel. Don't worry about saying it right or doing it right. God loves you and cares about your life.

2- **Call Someone:** You should have at least five people you can call at any time of the day or night. I recommend calling your 12 Step sponsor, pastor, supportive friend, spiritual mentor or counselor. It's best if you start calling a few of these people every day even when you're doing well. It gets you use to picking up that 50 pound telephone.

3- **Play the Movie to the end:** This is nothing more than consequential thinking. If your midbrain is trying to remember the good times of drinking a cold beer it's probably playing a movie in your head. It's trying to get you to think about all the fun and cool stuff from the past. While the movie is playing go ahead and play it to the end of the movie. You know, all the way to the county jail, to detox, to the hospital or a rehab center. Play it all the way to the parts that cause shame and guilt. Most of the time this will give you the courage to redirect your midbrain and get focused on something else, especially if you catch it early.

4- **Count back from 100:** Some people make fun of this one and say it sounds lame. Well, actually this is the one I get the most feedback from that works the best. The reason is because it's very difficult for you to focus on two different things at the same time. When you recognize the midbrains trick (thought, feeling, imagination) start counting backwards from 100 and you'll distract your thinking until you can get to the phone or a safer state of mind.

5- **Exercise:** This one works well when you recognize a feeling from your midbrain. Usually the feeling is stress or some kind of negative emotion and your Beast is screaming alcohol or drugs. Doing push-ups, going for a run or walk around the block or mow your lawn – anything to get those endorphins pumping and relieving that stress.

Like I said earlier, I encourage you to memorize these five techniques so you can combat your midbrain thoughts, feelings and imaginations to drink alcohol and use drugs.

Chapter 4:

The Humble Road to Recovery

A wise man once said that being humble in recovery is just as important as food and water is to the body. A humble spirit is one of the most important characteristics I look for in a person serious about change. I can't humble someone. If I tried to humble someone it would turn out to be humiliation and that never works. A person has to humble themselves. And that takes living a life of honesty.

I believe there are three rules of long term recovery: honesty, hard work and action. If you think you may be addicted to drugs or alcohol, the first thing you need to do is seek out advice and direction from an addiction specialist or medical professional. It's time to get honest about your using or drinking because withdrawal from drugs/alcohol is very dangerous; especially alcohol and benzo's. You may need to go through the detoxification process. Most hospitals and substance abuse counselors will give you an assessment and sometimes it's free.

Let's look at the three rules of recovery: Honesty, Hard Work and Action. You need to get honest with everyone in your life especially yourself. It's important to be open and honest with your inner circle; spouse, family and close friends. You also need to inform your doctor, dentist, pharmacist and pastor. Some of them can start becoming your support system. We'll talk more about that later in another chapter. The important thing at this point is getting honest with the people trying to support you.

Let's talk a little about being honest with the most important person - you. Most people get to the point in their addiction that they start lying and conning so much and for so long they start believing their own lies. That's when it gets really sick. I've seen people so deep into this personal deception they forget or don't know how to get out of their own spider web of lies. Getting out of this pit of dishonesty is important. You have to take a serious look at what you've been doing and take personal responsibility for your actions. This takes honesty and if done right, it will bring you to your knees. And this is the humble beginnings of change.

At this point, I encourage you to focus on one thing. Write, write and write some more. Please remember this – The more you write, the more you heal, and the more you heal, the better you feel.

The more you write about your life the more honest you'll become. I've listed five questions for you to consider. After you finish this book, take a notepad and answer these questions. It's important to get as detailed as possible. The more detailed answers you write down the healthier, honest and humble you'll become. This promotes long term sobriety – but it starts right here.

1. Write down your <u>entire</u> life history of using drugs and/or alcohol.

2. List <u>all</u> the problems using and drinking has caused you during your lifetime.

3. Write in <u>detail</u> all the problems using/drinking has caused all your family members.

4. Calculate how much money using/drinking has cost you in your <u>lifetime</u>.

5. Describe in <u>detail</u> your shame and guilt issues concerning using/drinking.

This is the second part of the three rules of recovery: Hard Work. It takes hard work to really do this assignment. I've had tough strong men cry like little babies getting honest about what they've put their families through. When you look in the mirror of honesty I want you to start saying to yourself, "I don't want to be this kind of person anymore. I don't want to be this way anymore. I want to be someone different. I want to change."

It takes hard work to get real about your emotions and then share them with others. It takes hard work to follow your recovery plan when you don't feel good. It takes hard work to be a man or woman of integrity and do what you say you're going to do. I've also found the harder you work on your recovery the easier it gets. But let me be quick to point out; at the beginning it's not easy – it's simple but not easy. It takes hard [honest] work. You've got to want it for you. Not for your family, your job or anything else. You've got to want it for yourself.

This is difficult for some people to understand. Your personal recovery has to come first. You cannot take care of your family if you're not clean and sober. It will take hard work [personal sacrifice] to work all day at your job, follow your recovery plan and then spend quality time with your family. This is why I almost entitled this book; Recovery Isn't For Cowards.

The third part of the three rules of recovery is Action. Action is the real power of this exercise. It will help you move along the humble road of recovery. As I mentioned earlier we've all heard that knowledge is power but I believe applied knowledge is the real power. The word power means the ability to take action or get something done. So, in order for any of this to be real in your life you have to apply the principles. You have to take action.

I've worked with people over the years that could quote the AA Big Book, the Bible and spew out recovery jargon from the last seven treatment centers but couldn't back any of it up with action. A wise man once said, "Faith without works is dead." A person full of pride and rebellion will not listen to instruction much less follow a detailed plan of action. But a person who is broken, sick-n-tired, humble, teachable and [ready to change] will listen to instruction, make a plan of action and follow this plan under the accountability of others – one day at a time.

Action really does separate the winners from the losers. Most losers quit. They quit on themselves, the program, their family and they quit on their purpose in life. This is a major character defect for a lot of people struggling with addiction. They do not finish what they start. Most of the people I've worked with during the years struggle with this negative trait. It's very important to start accomplishing small goals and sticking to what you say you're going to do.

You can start today by beginning the process of answering the five questions listed earlier. And remember ...

The More You Write

The More You Heal

&

The More You Heal

The Better You Feel

Chapter 5:

Courage, Integrity and Honor

I recognize some of you have courage, integrity and honor. The majority of you have demonstrated lots of courage just to survive the last several years. Many of you were taught by a family member, friend or coach what integrity really means. And some of you lived an honorable life with respect for yourself, your neighbor and family. However, most of you lost your courage, integrity and honor traveling down the rebellious road of addiction.

The past twenty years working with men and women struggling with addiction has taught me a few things but one stands out more than them all; in order to maintain long term sobriety you really need to allow God to help you develop the character traits of courage, integrity and honor.

Courage: The ability to take positive action in the face of danger, fear, death, pain and difficulty.

Integrity: The ability to act in accordance to your own values, morals and ethical principles.

Honor: The ability to act respectful toward and be honest with yourself, others and society.

Courage

It's going to take courage to tell your old friends you don't live that way anymore. For some of you, in order to let go of emotional scars from your past you'll have to face those bad memories. It takes courage to show your emotions in front of others. Some of you will have to find the courage to face your fears and deal with the issues that may be holding you back. Any coward can run and hide in a bottle or drug.

It takes courage to admit you can't do this alone and ask for help. Some of you are going to find this hard to do. Cowards don't ask for help. They think it's a sign of weakness. Actually it's the opposite. Strength is always in numbers. Three strings are stronger than one. One stick can be easily broken but five sticks are hard to break.

It's going to take personal courage to work hard all day at your job and then find the strength to attend a support group and then spend quality time with your family.

Ask God to give you the heart of a champion; the ability to be men and women that will not give up when times get tough.

Integrity

Almost everyone struggling with addiction has thrown their integrity out the window. Some of you had plenty of integrity but lost it to addiction which has a way of making you do things you normally wouldn't do. I always ask this question to my new clients. Has your behavior and choices over the last few years conflicted with your own morals and values? They all answer yes. When your behavior is contradicting your own values you'll have internal conflict. I call this spiritual cancer.

When you lack integrity your mouth will say one thing and your actions will say another. I encourage you to become men and women of integrity. Do what you say you're going to do. It's important to stick to your word. If you plan to attend church or make ninety 12 step meetings in ninety days – then do it. Don't make excuses and don't go back-in-forth like an irresponsible hypocrite. A wise man once said a double-minded man is unstable in all his ways.

Honor

Some of you need to start honoring authority. To be dishonorable is to disrespect the authority in your life. This goes back to the rebellious spirit and the need to humble yourself before your authorities. If you can do this then you can honor yourself and the important people in your life. Here is a spiritual truth: If you don't love yourself you can't love others. Honor is all about love. If you don't love yourself you won't respect yourself and you won't respect the ones who care about you. Learn how to love yourself.

When I was in the US Marine Corps we were taught to honor God, Country and The Marine Corps. If we submitted ourselves to God (The King) and honored him and served him then we would have a deep love for our country and our fellow marines. That kind of honor breads servanthood. Every US Marine understands how deep that honor runs.

You need to start honoring your sponsor, pastor, counselor, parents, probation officer and any authority in your life. Submit yourself to them and serve them with humility. The most important people you need to honor are your family. Be honest and respectful with your spouse and your children and serve them with all your heart.

I wish above all things that you decide today that you will live your life with courage, integrity and honor.

Chapter 6:

Developing a Recovery Plan

The late Father Martin and Doctor Bob said it best:

"Trust God, Clean House and Help Others."

Over the years I have counseled and interviewed thousands of individuals. These principles are a summary of what worked for most of them to overcome addiction. The majority of people I've worked with living successful lives free from addiction follow these simple principles.

Don't take this information lightly. Read and study each word. Follow these principles and you'll greatly increase your chances of success. It is possible for you to have peace of mind and a life of serenity.

1. **Make a commitment to not pick up the next drink or next drug today.**

Most people get frustrated and develop anxiety about the thoughts of NEVER being able to drink alcohol or use drugs again for the rest of their life. Well, stop right there. You need to learn how to live one day at a time. We're all only given a daily reprieve and even the Bible says we should only count today for tomorrow has enough struggles of it's own.

I use the word next because the next one is right around the corner waiting on you to have a thought, feeling or imagination to use?

So, don't worry about next week, the next cook-out, football game or holiday; just focus on not picking up that next one today. For some of you it'll be one minute or one hour at a time for a few days. But, if you don't take the next one you won't have to worry about all the rest. Like the old saying goes; one is too many and a thousand is never enough.

2. **Join a local 12 Step group, obtain a sponsor ASAP, work all the steps and get involved with the group. Or join an alternative support group and do the same.**

I believe some people don't need to attend 12 Step meetings and some people do. It's a personal decision whereby you need to be honest with yourself and the people trying to help you. If a person is in the "use" stage of walking down the road of addiction, he or she may not need to attend 12 step meetings. They usually just stop on their own and never use again. But, if you're in the abuse or dependence stage, you need to seriously consider getting involved in a good 12 step fellowship or alternative support group.

Some of you in the abuse stage would benefit from several meetings per week. If you're in the dependence stage (alcoholic/addict) you would greatly benefit from attending 90 meetings in 90 days and a serious commitment thereafter. I've also worked with very chronic people that needed to attend 12 Step meetings every day for the rest of their life or they would surely die. I encourage you to take a serious look at where you're at right now and what your behavior has been like for the past several years and make a decision about your involvement in support groups.

3. Stay away from all the old negative people, places and things.

There's an old sayings that goes like this: If you hang around the barber shop long enough you'll eventually get a haircut. I've seen a lot of folks leave recovery centers and get up from church alters with good intentions and go right back to the same old people, places and things. It's not long until they're using again. You really don't need to go see how Boo Boo or Curley or June Bug is doing. They're doing the same old wrong thing the same old wrong way. It's probably time for you to develop some new friends.

Now some of you had a few good friends and your addiction drove them away. If the truth be known, most people abusing drugs and alcohol don't have any true friends. You may have called them drinking or using buddies. Just understand it's very hard to go back around those old using friends and not be dragged down or caught in the trap. It's like a bucket full of crabs. They'll climb on top of each other trying to get out and when one gets close to the top another one will grab him trying to pull himself up and then pull him back down.

You need to also watch out for places that remind you of using and drinking. You can't go to the club and drink grapefruit juice with salt around the rim. You'll have too many triggers stirring up your midbrain beast. It's a trap, stay away from it like it's the plague.

I know some of you didn't do the bar or club thing. You probably isolated and drank or used alone. It doesn't take a rocket scientist to tell you that isolation is very dangerous. All of you should make some new friends and find healthy places to hang out. Most of you probably need to create a whole new life for yourself and your family.

4. Exercise at least three times per week (cardio workout).

The 12 Step fellowships tell us that resentments are the number one offender and cause of relapse. A recent study also conveys that stress is a major contributor for an alcoholic/addict to return back to alcohol and drugs. I'm assuming all of you understand the importance of how exercise can reduce stress.

If you cope with stress in a healthy way you'll greatly reduce your chances of relapse. I like to promote cardio workouts because it's important to get your heart beating faster. You can run, swim, walk around the block, join a gym, take up martial arts and/or just work in your yard. Just going outside helps because it gets you around people and you pick up some vitamin D from the sunshine. Exercise also produces endorphins which make you feel relaxed and calm.

5. Seek out a Higher Power and make a commitment to character building.

For some people, when you talk about a higher power they get a little freaked out. I'll try to keep this real simple too. A higher power is someone outside of yourself that you can lean on in the time of need. Someone you can trust for advice, correction, love and friendship. I'm not talking about God, your eternal savior (but it can be), I'm talking more like a group of people. The 12 Step fellowships can be your higher power for a while until you find your spiritual awakening and build your foundation.

I understand that a person can get sober and clean without a higher power. I've witnessed it many times. However, there's an old saying that goes like this; what do you get when you sober up a drunken horse thief -- a horse thief. You'll need to start allowing people and mainly God to work on your character issues. Father Martin called it *cleaning house*.

Like I said earlier, anyone can stop drinking and drugging, that's easy. The hard part is staying clean and sober. This is my definition of recovery: Recovery is living life on life's terms without turning to a mood altering chemical. The reason most people need a higher power is to learn how to live life without a mood altering chemical.

A higher power is needed to learn how to live a successful life. Most of you need to learn how to be a responsible parent, spouse, friend, neighbor and citizen. It'll take some humbleness to admit it. Go ahead and admit it — we need each other and especially God to survive and thrive in this journey called life.

6. Volunteer your time serving others as often as possible.

I often have clients, and it's usually after a spiritual awakening, tell me they want to serve God or become a counselor or minister. I always tell them the same thing: If you want to serve God, serve people and if you want to love God, love people.

It helps you get out of self when you serve others by donating your time, energy and resources. Most people struggling with addiction have a tendency to be selfish. When you help others it also reminds you that your life may not be that bad after all.

You can serve in your neighborhood, community, church and if you're working your recovery program correctly you should be doing some service work in your 12 Step fellowship. This is the *helping others* part that Father Martin spoke about in his lectures.

7. Receive professional counseling services.

Some of you need to visit with a professional counselor while others may not need this service. I encourage all of you to at least meet once or twice with a licensed therapist for an assessment. You and the therapist can determine after the assessment if their services will be beneficial for you and your family.

Some people start using drugs to self-medicate and/or mask a painful experience from the past. Trauma is a silent killer. For most people it takes a while to get over a past hurt. Some hurts go deep and you may need more than a sponsor, pastor, friend or family member. Some pastors are not trained in the mental health field and your family and friends don't need to take on this role; it's not fair to them either.

Some of you would benefit from marriage and family counseling. Your spouse and children have been through a lot of emotional struggles with you. This may save your family – try it.

8. Find new recreational activities and have some fun.

It's also important to make time for fun and recreation. Find some new activities or return to the healthy fun stuff you use to do before drugs and alcohol took over your life. Start planning fun indoor and outdoor recreational activities with your family and positive friends. Life is good today. The sober and clean life is awesome. Get out there and get you some of this new clean and sober life. It's a blast!

Final Words:

Well, that's it folks. I hope this little book helps you. I've seen a lot of people overcome addiction and do very well in life. So, be encouraged and hopeful. Stay focused and surrender to the program. It works if you work it so work it every day.

I've also included, after my acknowledgment, a copy of my original workbook. I hope you can read it.

God bless you and your family.

Acknowledgement

There are a lot of people I would like to thank for encouraging me to write this little workbook. My clients are always telling me I should write a book or make a video and share my stuff. Well, I finally listened to them and here it is. It's small, but it's my heart beat concerning the field of addiction and recovery.

I would also like to thank my wonderful wife. She has always been there for me and never gave up on me. She has always encouraged me to chase my dreams: Thank you sweetheart.

I would also like to thank my mother. She always demonstrates a can-do attitude and a life of perseverance. She's been blind in one eye since a teenager, endured a heart-breaking divorce in her thirties, had two hip replacements in her forties and fifties and survived breast cancer in her sixties. She is a winner and she taught me the importance of never giving up and keeping a positive attitude.

I would also like to acknowledge a few past co-workers and counseling professionals that made a big difference in my career: Casey Corbin, Tom Lorraine, Bobby Buck, Tim Riser, William Vargas, Bethany Dollar, Carol Aldrich-George, Gloria Jones, John Raymond and the late Father Martin.

The most important of all is my Lord and savior Jesus Christ.

You can contact me for additional information, company trainings, conference lectures or coaching services at:

workwithdallas@gmail.com

All the art work in my original workbook was drawn by a former patient whom I have grown to consider a friend and brother.
Semper Fi – Chris H. 2010

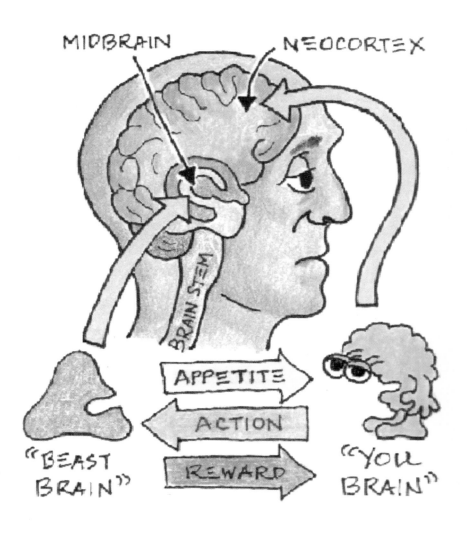

HOW A "NORMAL" PERSON'S BRAIN WORKS

REMEMBER, YOUR "BEAST BRAIN" AND "YOU BRAIN" WORK AS A TEAM TO HELP YOU SURVIVE.

HERE'S THE "BEAST BRAIN'S" "PUMP" OF CHEMICALS IT USES TO SEND SIGNALS TO THE "YOU BRAIN"

THIS FUNNEL REPRESENTS HOW THE "YOU" BRAIN" RECEIVES THOSE CHEMICALS.

"PLEASURE METER"

SO, YOUR MIDBRAIN DECIDES YOU NEED FOOD:

Hey, a little dopamine if you score us a cheeseburger!

Burger-got it.

VALUES: A BURGER NOW & THEN IS OK.
THINK: SURE WOULD TASTE GOOD
DECIDE: OK, LET'S EAT!
ACT: • GET CAR KEYS & MONEY
• DRIVE TO FAST-FOOD JOINT
• ORDER #2 AND EAT

Good job! Here's a reward. Keep it up!

DOPAMINE

Mmm, tasty.

CONSEQUENCES
• NOT HUNGRY ANYMORE
• BURGER TASTED GOOD
• A BIT OF NOURISHMENT.
• SPENT $5.49
• BACK IN TIME TO GET KIDS.

We make a good team.

I agree

SO:
THE "BEAST BRAIN" CAN'T SEE, HAS NO ARMS OR LEGS, AND HAS NO INTELLIGENCE OF IT'S OWN. BUT IT ENLISTS THE "YOU BRAIN'S" THOUGHTS AND INTELLIGENCE, SEES THROUGH YOUR EYES, CREATES STRONG FEELINGS AND PERSUADES YOU TO USE YOUR HANDS, ARMS, AND LEGS TO GET WHAT YOUR BODY NEEDS. IT ALL NORMALLY WORKS WELL.

4

HOW A PERSON GETS ADDICTED

ALL DRUGS DIRECTLY OR INDIRECTLY REWARD THE "YOU BRAIN" WITH **DOPAMINE**, WHICH CAUSES **PHYSICAL PLEASURE**. WHEN YOU USE, THE "BEAST BRAIN" FLOODS THE "YOU BRAIN" WITH MUCH MORE DOPAMINE THAN IT DOES TO REWARD NORMAL BEHAVIOR. THIS MAKES YOU FEEL EUPHORIA, AND TEACHES YOU TO KEEP USING DRUGS.

5

WHAT HAPPENS TO AN ADDICTED BRAIN?

① You DEPLETE THE NOR-
MAL LEVELS OF CHEMICALS
IN YOUR "BEAST BRAIN'S"
"PUMP." WITHOUT THE
DRUGS OR ALCOHOL, YOU
CAN'T GET THE NORMAL
EFFECT OF THESE CHEMICALS.

② IN RESPONSE TO SUCH
UNNATURAL LEVELS OF
DOPAMINE & OTHER CHEM-
ICALS, YOUR BRAIN ACTU-
ALLY **REDUCES ITS CAPACITY
TO RECEIVE** THEM — IN
ESSENCE, YOUR "FUNNEL"
GETS SMALLER.

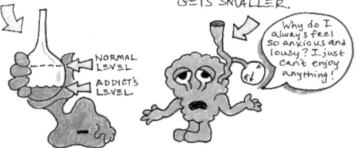

NORMAL
LEVEL

ADDICT'S
LEVEL

Why do I
always feel
so anxious and
lousy? I just
can't enjoy
anything!

THUS, THINGS YOU ONCE FOUND PLEASURABLE DON'T
MAKE YOU FEEL AS GOOD ANYMORE. _OR_, IF YOU'RE
STILL USING, YOUR **TOLERANCE** GOES UP — IT TAKES
MORE AND MORE TO GET YOU HIGH. IF YOU STOP USING
IT WILL TAKE ABOUT **6-12 MONTHS FOR YOUR BRAIN TO HEAL.**

③ BUT... HERE'S THE REALLY **BAD
NEWS** - YOUR MIDBRAIN HAS BEEN
PERMANENTLY REPROGRAMMED
TO TRY AND TRICK YOU INTO US-
ING, AND WILL DO SO FOR THE
REST OF YOUR LIFE. YOUR BRAIN
WILL ALWAYS REMEMBER WHAT
IT'S LIKE TO GET HIGH. (BUT DON'T WORRY, WE'LL DISCUSS
THE GOOD NEWS LATER!)

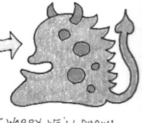

6

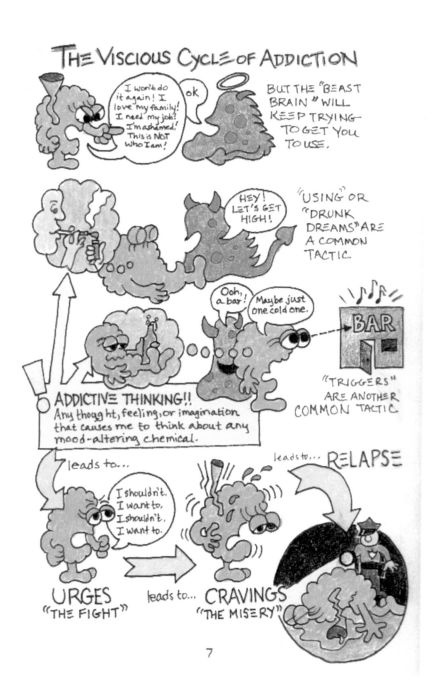

WHY IS IT HARD TO BREAK THE CYCLE?

ADDICTIVE THINKING ⟹ URGE ⟹ CRAVING ⟹ **RELAPSE**

Fantasizing "Romancing"

"It would be nice..."

The Fight

"Should I or shouldn't I?"

The Misery

"I want to sooo bad..."

The Obsession

"How did this happen again?"

THE REALITY FOR ADDICTS & ALCOHOLICS IS THAT UNLESS THEY LEARN TO RECOGNIZE ADDICTIVE THINKING AND TAKE **IMMEDIATE ACTION** TO IGNORE THEIR "BEAST BRAIN," THEY ARE **VERY** LIKELY TO USE. WHY?

BECAUSE IT'S JUST ABOUT IMPOSSIBLE FOR YOUR "YOU BRAIN" TO WIN AN ARGUMENT WITH YOUR "BEAST BRAIN." HERE'S WHY:

① YOUR "BEAST BRAIN" HAS A "COMMUNICATION SUPERHIGHWAY" TO THE "YOU BRAIN," ITS MESSAGES TRAVEL VERY FAST.

② REMEMBER THAT AS YOUR BRAIN LEARNS TO REPEAT PLEASURABLE BEHAVIOR, IT REWIRES ITSELF TO CREATE "DIRECT LINES" BACK TO THE "BEAST BRAIN." IF YOU MOMENTARILY GIVE IN AND SAY "YES," THAT MESSAGE GETS TO THE "BEAST BRAIN" PRETTY QUICKLY COMPARED TO OTHER BRAIN MESSAGES.

③ IF YOUR "YOU BRAIN" DECIDES "NO" TO USING, THAT MESSAGE MUST TRAVEL ALONG THE "BACK ROADS" OF YOUR BRAIN'S WIRING. IT GETS TO THE "BEAST BRAIN" COMPARATIVELY SLOWLY. BY THAT TIME, YOUR "BEAST BRAIN" HAS SENT SEVERAL MORE "USE!" MESSAGES TO YOUR "YOU BRAIN." AND REMEMBER, NORMALLY YOUR SURVIVAL DEPENDS ON YOUR "YOU BRAIN" DOING WHAT THE "BEAST BRAIN" SAYS.

④ AND FINALLY, YOUR "BEAST BRAIN" **NEVER** GIVES UP!

BUT THERE IS A SOLUTION! ⟹

8

BREAKING THE CYCLE IS SIMPLE —
BUT NOT EASY

BOTTOM LINE: IF YOU CAN'T WIN AN ARGUMENT WITH YOUR "BEAST BRAIN," THEN DON'T ARGUE WITH IT – IGNORE IT! **AS SOON AS YOU RECOGNIZE ADDICTIVE THINKING (R.A.T.), TAKE IMMEDIATE ACTION** TO MAKE YOUR "YOU BRAIN" THINK ABOUT SOMETHING ELSE. IT'S ALMOST IMPOSSIBLE FOR YOUR "YOU BRAIN" TO THINK ABOUT TWO THINGS AT THE SAME TIME. HERE ARE **FIVE THINGS <u>PROVEN</u> TO WORK:**

ADDICTIVE THINKING
Any thought, feeling, or imagination that causes me to think about any mood-altering chemical.

1. CALL SOMEONE.
2. PRAY
3. "PLAY THE MOVIE TO THE END"
4. COUNT BACKWARDS FROM 100
5. EXERCISE

THAT'S IT? YES – IT'S THAT SIMPLE. BUT YOU HAVE TO TAKE ACTION NOW, EVEN IF YOU DON'T FEEL LIKE IT. DON'T WAIT FOR THE DESIRE TO USE TO GO AWAY. THIS IS WHERE **PERSONAL RESPONSIBILITY** KICKS IN. YOU'RE NOT RESPONSIBLE FOR THE FIRST THOUGHT, BUT YOU ARE FOR THE SECOND. TRAIN YOURSELF TO **USE THE R.A.T. TECHNIQUE** TO COMBAT YOUR "BEAST BRAIN." HUMBLE YOURSELF TO DO IT!

AFTER A WHILE, THE FEROCIOUS "BARKING DOG" OF YOUR "BEAST BRAIN" WILL DIE DOWN DOWN TO A CHIHUAHUA.

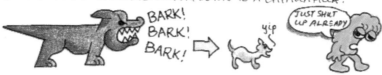

9

ADDICTION AS A DISEASE

NOT EVERYONE WHO USES OR EVEN ABUSES DRUGS OR ALCOHOL BECOMES ADDICTED; BUT MANY DO. SCIENTISTS BELIEVE THAT GENETICS ACCOUNT FOR 40-60% OF A PERSON'S VULNERABILITY TO ADDICTION, WITH ENVIRONMENTAL FACTORS MAKING UP THE DIFFERENCE.

INVISIBLE LINE OF ADDICTION:
COMPULSIVE DRUG-SEEKING & USE
DESPITE HARMFUL CONSEQUENCES

	USE ──▶	ABUSE ──▶	DEPENDENCE
DAMAGE	SPIRITUAL SOCIAL	PSYCHOLOGICAL: DEPRESSION, ANXIETY, ETC.	BIOLOGICAL: PERMANENT BRAIN DAMAGE
TREATMENT	STOP	OUTPATIENT	INPATIENT
LENGTH OF TREATMENT	6-12 MONTHS TO BUILD SPIRITUAL FOUNDATION	6-12 MONTHS TO DEAL WITH ANXIETY, SHAME, ETC.	6-12 MONTHS FOR BRAIN TO REPAIR ITSELF (some damage permanent)

◀── **18 MONTHS TO 3 YEARS** ──▶
TO BUILD A SOLID FOUNDATION
OF SOBRIETY OR CLEAN TIME

AS WE'VE ALREADY SEEN, ONCE A PERSON BECOMES CHEMICALLY DEPENDENT, THE PRIMARY PROBLEM IN THEIR CONDITION IS PHYSICAL DAMAGE TO THE MOST COMPLEX ORGAN — THE BRAIN. THUS, ADDICTION IS SIMILAR TO OTHER CHRONIC DISEASES SUCH AS TYPE II DIABETES OR HEART DISEASE, WHICH ALSO ARE CAUSED OR MADE WORSE BY GENETIC, ENVIRONMENTAL, AND BEHAVIORAL FACTORS.

FOR THESE REASONS, THE PREVAILING SCIENTIFIC VIEW (AND THAT OF THE FEDERAL GOVERNMENT) IS THAT ADDICTION IS A **CHRONIC, PROGRESSIVE**, AND (IF UNTREATED) **FATAL** DISEASE.

10

CHRONIC.

ADDICTION IS A **LIFE-LONG DISEASE.** ONCE YOU REACH THE DEPENDENCY STAGE, YOUR BRAIN HAS BEEN PERMANENTLY ALTERED - YOUR "BEAST BRAIN" PERMA- NENTLY REPROGRAMMED. FOR THIS REASON, ADDICTS AND ALCOHOLICS RUN A VERY HIGH RISK OF **CROSS-ADDICTION** - IN SHORT, SWAPPING OUT YOUR "PROBLEM DRUG" WITH ONE YOU THINK IS NOT A PROBLEM, ONLY TO FIND YOUR- SELF JUST AS DEPENDENT ON THE NEW SUBSTANCE. THIS IS A DANGEROUS TRAP. AN ADDICT CAN NEVER SAFELY USE A MOOD-ALTERING CHEMICAL UNLESS UNDER THE CARE OF A DOCTOR.

PROGRESSIVE.

ADDICTION ALWAYS GETS WORSE OVER TIME. EVEN AFTER AN ADDICT HAS BEEN CLEAN FOR A LONG TIME - EVEN YEARS - AS SOON AS THEY PICK-UP AGAIN, THEIR ADDICTION QUICKLY PROGRESSES TO WHERE IT LEFT-OFF, AND THEN GETS WORSE. THE CHART BELOW SHOWS THE PROGRESSION OF AN ACTUAL GREENLEAF PATIENT.*

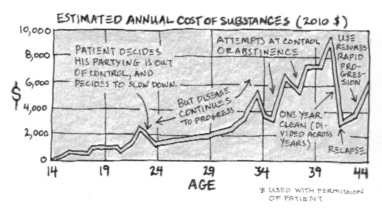

ESTIMATED ANNUAL COST OF SUBSTANCES (2010 $)

* USED WITH PERMISSION OF PATIENT

FATAL.

LEFT UNTREATED, **ADDICTION IS FATAL** - EITHER THROUGH OVERDOSE, ACCIDENT WHILE INTOXICATED, VIOLENCE, OR HEALTH PROBLEMS CAUSED BY THE ADDICTION.

//

53

ADDICTION AS AN "ALLERGY"

WHEN ALCOHOLICS ANONYMOUS (A.A.) WAS FORMING IN THE MID-1930'S, DR. WILLIAM SILKWORTH, WHO HAD TREATED MANY ALCOHOLICS, CONCLUDED THAT ALCOHOLISM IS AN ALLERGY, WHICH SOME PEOPLE HAVE FROM BIRTH AND OTHERS DEVELOP LATER. HIS VIEW IS EXPRESSED IN THE SECTION ENTITLED "THE DOCTOR'S OPINION" IN THE A.A. "BIG BOOK."

CONSIDER PEOPLE WITH HAY FEVER — AN ALLERGY TO CERTAIN TYPES OF POLLEN. SOME PEOPLE HAVE IT FROM BIRTH, BUT MANY PEOPLE DEVELOP THE ALLERGY ONLY AFTER PROLONGED EXPOSURE OVER MANY YEARS. **ONCE THEY HAVE THE ALLERGY, THEY HAVE IT FOR LIFE.** WHILE THEY MOVE TO A NEW STATE AND HAVE NO SYMPTOMS FOR MANY YEARS, ONCE THEY ARE RE-EXPOSED TO THE POLLEN, THEY HAVE AN ALLERGIC REACTION AS STRONG OR STRONGER THAN BEFORE.

ACHOO!

Exposure to Substance

Abnormal Reaction

IN MEDICAL TERMS, ADDICTION ISN'T REALLY AN ALLERGY BECAUSE IT'S A PROBLEM OF THE BRAIN, NOT THE IMMUNE SYSTEM. BUT **THE ANALOGY IS VERY SIMPLE AND USEFUL.**

IF YOU'RE ALLERGIC TO EGGS, YOU DON'T EAT EGGS. **IF YOU'RE ALLERGIC TO ALCOHOL OR DRUGS, YOU DON'T DRINK OR USE!** IT'S THAT SIMPLE!

MORE MORE!

Exposure to Substance

Abnormal Reaction

12

FEELINGS AND EMOTIONS

IN ADDITION TO DOPAMINE, ALCOHOL AND DRUGS MESS WITH MANY
OTHER BRAIN CHEMICALS, ALL OF WHICH HAVE **PROFOUND IMPACTS
ON YOUR FEELINGS AND EMOTIONS — WHILE USING AND IN RECOVERY.**

HERE ARE SOME OF THE MOST IMPORTANT BRAIN CHEMICALS
THAT ARE BLOCKED, OVERUSED, OR DEPLETED BY USING:

CHEMICAL	NATURAL FUNCTION	INTERFERED WITH BY:
Dopamine	Reward, Pleasure	Cocaine, Alcohol, Nicotine, Marijuana
Serotonin	Calmness, Sleep, Sadness	Alcohol, Sleeping Pills, Marijuana
Endorphin	Pain Relief	Pain Pills, Nicotine, Self-Mutilation
GABA	Anti-Anxiety	Cocaine, Meth, Ecstasy, Alcohol
Epinephrine	Anger, Fear, Fight-or-Flight	Meth, Cocaine, Alcohol
PIP	Caring, Love, Relationship	Cocaine, Meth, Alcohol, Chocolate

TAKE ALCOHOL FOR AN EXAMPLE. WHEN DRINKING, DOPAMINE PRO-
DUCES EUPHORIA AND SEROTONIN PRODUCES FEELINGS OF WELL-
BEING. WHEN AN ALCOHOLIC STOPS DRINKING, IT TAKES TIME FOR
THESE CHEMICALS TO RETURN TO NORMAL LEVELS. IN ADDI-
TION, G.A.B.A. DROPS AND NOREPINEPHRINE INCREASES,
CAUSING INTENSE AGITATION, STRESS, AND IMPULSIVITY.

WHEN YOU STOP USING, EXPECT AN EMOTIONAL **ROLLER-COASTER**
RIDE LASTING MONTHS OR YEARS. THIS IS WHY RECOVERING ALCOHOL-
ICS RECOMMEND NO RELATIONSHIPS OR BIG DECISIONS FOR ONE YEAR.

13

III. THE CHALLENGE: STAYING CLEAN & SOBER

SUCCESFUL RECOVERY IS BUILT ON THREE PILLARS, ALL OF WHICH REST ON A FOUNDATION OF HARD WORK, HONESTY, & ACTION.

SOBER & CLEAN

DEVELOP A SOLID SUPPORT NETWORK

1. **ACCOUNTABILITY**
   - Sponsor
   - Life Coach
   - Supportive Friend
   - Spiritual Mentor

2. **STRUCTURE**
   - Routines
   - Positive Habits
   - Keep Busy!

3. **SUPPORT**
   - AA or NA
   - Celebrate Recovery
   - Outpatient Counseling
   - Church

RECOGNIZE & SILENCE YOUR BEAST

1. **RECOGNIZE ADDICTIVE THINKING**

2. **TAKE IMMEDIATE ACTION**
   - Pray
   - Call someone
   - Play the movie to the end.
   - Count backwards from 100
   - Exercise

FOLLOW YOUR RELAPSE PREVENTION PLAN

1. **COMMIT** to not drink or drug - today
2. **JOIN** a support group
3. **AVOID** negative people, places, things
4. **EXERCISE** - cardio; 3 times per week
5. **SEEK** a Higher Power and make a commitment to build your character.
6. **VOLUNTEER** serving others.
7. **RECEIVE** professional counseling
8. **FIND** new activities and **HAVE FUN**

HARD WORK ~ HONESTY ~ ACTION

Just Say No

Remember These Two Things:

1. EVERYONE STARTS USING DRUGS AND ALCOHOL FOR ONE REASON — TO CHANGE THEIR MOOD.

2. EVERYONE STOPS USING DRUGS AND ALCOHOL THE SAME WAY — BY NOT TAKING THE NEXT ONE.

IT'S THAT SIMPLE. IT'S NOT EASY — BUT IT'S SIMPLE.

Very Important:

I NEED TO ACCEPT THE FACT I CAN NOT DRINK ALCOHOL OR USE DRUGS LIKE EVERYONE ELSE, MAKE A COMMITMENT TO ABSTINENCE AND MOVE ON WITH MY LIFE OR...

I WILL GO BACK INTO THE LABORATORY OF LIFE, CONDUCT SOME MORE DRINKING AND DRUGGING EXPERIMENTS, CAUSE SOME MORE PAIN, AND HOPEFULLY PROVE TO MYSELF I CANNOT DRINK OR USE DRUGS LIKE EVERYONE ELSE.

IF YOU SEE IT AS PLEASURABLE, YOU WILL DO IT.

IF YOU SEE IT AS PAINFUL, YOU WILL NOT DO IT.

23

Purchase additional copies of this book at:

MidbrainBeast.com

**ISBN-13:
978-1491232477**

**ISBN-10:
1491232471**

Made in the USA
Columbia, SC
01 December 2019